T0368707

BLOOD FEATHER

BLOOD FEATHER

Patrick McGuinness

CAPE POETRY

1 3 5 7 9 10 8 6 4 2

Jonathan Cape, an imprint of Vintage, is part of the Penguin Random House group of companies whose addresses can be found at global.penguinrandomhouse.com

Copyright © Patrick McGuinness 2023

Patrick McGuinness has asserted his right to be identified as the author of this Work in accordance with the Copyright, Designs and Patents Act 1988

First published by Jonathan Cape in 2023

penguin.co.uk/vintage

A CIP catalogue record for this book is available from the British Library

ISBN 9780224098311

Typeset in 11/13pt Bembo Book MT Pro by Jouve (UK), Milton Keynes
Printed and bound in Great Britain by TJ Books Limited, Padstow, Cornwall

The authorised representative in the EEA is Penguin Random House Ireland, Morrison Chambers, 32 Nassau Street, Dublin D02 YH68

Penguin Random House is committed to a sustainable future for our business, our readers and our planet. This book is made from Forest Stewardship Council® certified paper.

Moy qui fais profession de choses muettes

I who make profession of mute things

Poussin

CONTENTS

I
SQUEEZE THE DAY

IN THE ENGLISHMAN'S HOME

Little castles of milk teeth,
lined up to guard the helpless tongue –

sometimes dry as the clapper of a bell,
sometimes fat and lashing in its ditch –

it's where you kept the language you arrived with.
You hid it all that time and now it's gone.

NEW ACCENT

The new accent is a brace,
doing its slow work on your mouth.
At night you take it out to let your tongue
go dreaming outside its cage.

MOTHER AS BIRD

If she were a bird, she'd be the sparrow:
everywhere at once and then gone in one go.

She left in her hundreds, left me alone in her thousands,
and when her wings opened they closed the sky.

TIRED METAPHOR

When she died, I saw the river of death
I'd read about in books:
the books that didn't help,
then helped because they helped me see
there was no help in a river of ink.

I stood on the bank
and watched death sip from the tributary
of her dying; saw it flex a little
and swell at her addition –
a ridge in the dark cream of the water –

then smooth itself out and roll on.

TODAY IS ALREADY OVER

She is the ghost in my habits:
the way she cleared up around me –
not after me but before.
Removing my traces as I went,
she showed me my steps disappearing
in time to my walking,
my prints blanking over and the path
always turning the corner.

I'd leave a book open –
within minutes it was closed;
a plate of food taken as I ate.
When I bought the newspaper,
she threw it out by midday.
Dis! mon journal! I called out;
Le jour est fini, she replied,
the *ping* of the pedal-bin lid
against white kitchen tile:
something else heading down the chute
the rest of us called *now*.

The day is already over, she said
and she meant it.
She broke the tenses inside me,
made me live like I was evaporating:
told me I would never be
my own contemporary.

MOTHER AS SPY

All of our words for spying are taken
from the dictionary of sleep;
though it is the spy who is awake,
and the world around her sleeps.

This is my life, she thinks, *I am in deep cover,*
embedded in my motherhood, my marriage,
the things they see but which I'm something other
than. We eat and sleep and breathe and age

together – he and I; me and him;
the neighbours and me with our smiles.
I wait in lines. I taxi the children
from accomplishment to small

accomplishment. I cheer on touchlines.
I watch their hidden teenage lives
make smoke in the mirror as I drive.
They think because they're new to lies

it means I must be too. They cultivate
their own things which they learn to hide.
At first it's hard, because lying is to push a large thing
through a small hole in the language.

I am always waiting for the call.
When it comes, will I recognise the voice?
Was there a password?
I think my handler may have died;

been purged.

MOTHER AS HOSTAGE

On the phone she says *yes, yes, I'm OK*;
she sounds bored, sounds groggy, sounds both;
she talks in tired bounces like she's bumping
along the ground, a balloon sighing
as it shrinks to wrinkles.

I think she's reading from a script:
Yes they are treating me well, she says,
but it's hard to hear because she holds her face
too far from the receiver, as if she's looking at it
and is puzzled; or holding me and is puzzled
that all that's left of me is this: a voice.

Yes, she says, *oui. Non. Ça va.*
She's ticking off the answers.
I know I'm ticking off the questions.
Is it the drugs, I wonder, or the illness?

Though I should know by now
they're both the same,
just another suburban couple:
an illness married to a drug.

FAMILY AS FAILED STATE

Once the metaphor's in place
every day's a poem here
in the banana republic of blood.

MOTHER AS NOVEL

Lately, I've used the things I've read in novels
about people who were alone but married
and who were quietly extreme.

But unlike in books she didn't have the words
to say it all, there was no phone to dial 999
and ask for a narrator –

'Which service do you wish to be connected to?
First-person, third-person, reliable or unreliable?'

'Omniscient please. *Please.*'

– no one to help her to be seen by others,
to be heard; to mine her life for meanings
she was always on the other side of.

Now, on the other side of her, I imagine her
alone and childless, the girl and boy at school,
moving carefully among shadows
thick as the knots in water where currents meet.
Until he came back, drunk or yet to drink,
to a house where the hours
bled into each other like concussion.

The only time there was was him
and the clock's hands were his hands as they struck.

SURE THINGS

I start to tell myself the things I know
(well, the few things I'm still sure of):
poles in the swamp where I can build
the place I'll stay my mind; the jetty
where I'll moor it when I sleep,
and which I'll aim for when I wake.

But as I tell myself those things
I know them less,
and when I speak them out
I do not know who's speaking.

MOTHER AS PERFUME

On either side of Nina Ricci's *l'Air du Temps*
was the perfume that her body made around it:

hours old on the skin it was unmistakable –
top-note tobacco, base-note fear.
Sometimes it was the other way around,
the scent capsizing so the fear came first.

Decades later it's still there on her scarf,
an echo down the tunnel as I breathe it in:
still catching on the air as she leaves.

Scent is what's caught as it goes, scent is the going:
the turn of the shoulder, the swing of the door,
the *sillage*, the vapour-trail, the dissolving wake;
the smoke of the candle is the shadow of its flame.

A VISIT TO THE MUSEUM

She told me Rodin's *Thinker* was *l'homme qui pleure*.
Her jokes were a sweet dark syrup:
Rodin's *Weeper*.

Mais c'est l'Penseur! I corrected once I'd looked it up.
C'est pour ça qu'il pleure, she answered.
That shut me up.

MOTHER AS WIDOW

The barely-perceptible drag
of the marriage she carried:
like a bird who'd been tagged
and who flew with the weight
of its near-weightless ring.

CHILD-NARRATOR

I said I was too young to work
in the factory for sad thoughts;
told her my sorrows were entry-level
and I didn't have the words for hers.
But she promoted me to foreman,
made me her narrator
before I could become my own.

She taught me the numb, maladroit snippets
of translationese I spoke at school
and still speak now when I forget:
ready-meal phrases that never said
quite what she meant, then subsided
into saying more – they cast the shade
so wide of what they failed to say.

Sometimes she skewered me with pangs
of *mot juste*; taught me things
so correct no native would say them –
idioms she picked up in period dramas
and what she called *les feuilletons*
in the black hole of daytime TV.
The subjunctive. Phrases like *send for*,
words like *lest* and *wherefore*.

In company I was ashamed of her accent.
I laughed along with the others as I hid my own.
But my laughter reached her umbilically,
the sonar of my distancing only she could hear.

Most of what she meant stayed behind her eyes,
and every now and then came out as tears
that rolled singly down her cheek;
I am still bent around their curves.

ECT

After the sessions she was a broken wall:
the pieces of her, stacked and slotted;
haphazard, gappy. She only stood
because the wind blew through her

and not against. When she spoke
her voice came from some far-off
dry-stone moorland where it echoed
across the acres razed inside her head.

English Conversion Therapy, the children said:
mother reprogrammed, factory settings.
Soon she grew back, the gaps closed up.
She mortared herself together with remembering,

then toppled once more with its weight.

CLACKMUIR

She was *claquemurée*, she said.
Clackmuir is what I heard.
I thought she'd gone to Scotland.

She called from wall-mounted
phones in corridors
where the receiver was always warm,

the mouthpiece spittle-foamy,
her voice faint as they built the room
around her, painted institution

not-quite-white and easy-wipe
eggshell gloss. I heard the food sweat
through its plastic, smelled

the bleach-and-bucket marinade
of mops. I heard the clip of brick
on brick, the clack of stone on stone:

Claque claque, she whispered, *'y a pas d'clé* –
immured, enmured, clackmured –
there was no key she told me –

'y a pas d'porte non plus –
and soon there was no door.

claquemurer (Fr.): to shut away, immure

AT THE BACK OF THE PAINTING

She wants to be at the back of the painting:
some place up the disappearing path
where a woman washes in clear water,
where a cobalt cloth hangs
from the window of a house
three leagues deep into the canvas,
into the idea of space.

On hot days the water in the lipped jug
is as cool as clay
and braids in its pouring
from the deep into the light.

She tracks the path to where
the little dog is heading now,
where the sheep glaze
over in contemplation,
and the spiral staircase
folds its way into the night.
She's looking for the place
where it all stops: the dark window
from which she will pour,
endless in her freefall, her robe
a fluted line of white.

SQUEEZE THE DAY

is how I heard the line the first time around:
Carpe diem, *Squeeze the day*, I told them proudly.

The language of juicing seemed right for Horace,
and though my version amounted to more or less

the same, it had a better ring,
more urgent, and *squeeze* was closer

to what I wanted but didn't have the words for;
or what my body wanted, at school, at home,

and my body had not yet spoken to my mind:
because squeezing was to seize and to be seized

in return, to have the day seize you.
But when I learned what Horace really said,

when at last the day was there for squeezing,
it was dry.

VISITING HOUR

some way after Virgil's Aeneid VI

They medicate on thoughts of endings,
far from the speeches about existence
and oblivion: the pain that merely purls
around the words for pain,
that threads the therapeutic garlands
of the talking cure.

They speak in all they turn away from,
the grammar of the averted gaze:
Dido turning from Aeneas, the look
that asks the living why we still haunt the dead,
why we still hunt them down
into the shadows of their days.

LA MER

La mer/ Les a bercés . . .
Charles Trenet

In the pool, in the bath, head
underwater, or shell to your ear:
it's your umbilical heart you're hearing –
beating its retreat back to her.

MOTHER AS MIRROR

Always I've had that feeling,
looking at her photograph,
that I was the illusion
enamelled in the night sky of her eyes
– the fleeting light, the bled-out line –
and she the solid, rooted one,
still watching.

FACTORY FOR SAD THOUGHTS

Some days I become a factory for sad thoughts. As I turn in, the lights come on for the night shift. I used to make them by hand, the sad thoughts, but lately it's become more of an assembly line, the machines doing all the work: I sleep, and in the morning I have another consignment ready for distribution; for export, for import. It's hard to keep up with my own demand.

The last time my mother died, the final time – as she would have said, 'une fois pour toutes', once and for all – I was in Tenerife. She didn't speak much even when she was alive, so was certainly not going to waste the little she had to say on last words. So I had to make them up, not the words so much as the movement of the lips. Because even alive she was hard to read, abrupt and closed; an ocean's worth of storm closed inside an oyster.

One of the sad thoughts I manufacture is that I am trying to hear her speak, but, like in a bad film, the words and the movements of the mouth are out of sync. In the scenario I've constructed – her trying to say her last things to me – it causes me terrible anxiety, and I try to align her lips with the words she's speaking. It takes so much effort that I forget to hear the words themselves, and I'm not even sure they are words and in what language.

I get closer and closer, only to find it's a dark and ashy language, all muffled, and so low it's almost a growl. If those are the last words, I think to myself (my dream-self thinks to itself), I'm not sure I want to hear them.

I could perhaps trace this dream to the fact that she spoke French and was ill at ease with English. But even that doesn't explain it, because we spoke to each other in French always. Really the dream is about distance. In my dream she speaks, and the words overlap with the lips and then the lips outpace the words. There's the feeling of something lost in the crevasse, and it's all to do with time, with aligning two sets of moments, and I know that if I don't align them I will never hear, let alone understand. But maybe that is all she has to say anyway, all she wants me to understand. What she has to say she will show, not tell.

In French, the word for *dubbing* is *doublage*. When I speak it is her subtitles that beat beneath my voice.

Of all the poems I've ever written, this is the one I didn't.

II

THE NOISES THINGS MAKE
WHEN THEY LEAVE

POETRY

In *Singin' in the Rain*, Debbie Reynolds plays a woman with a good voice who replaces the beautiful silent-screen star Lina Lamont, who is grating and vulgar and is about to be vocally unmasked by the arrival of sound. The elocution lessons don't work and she can't lip-sync; you can't teach class, the film tells us, and class is authenticity.

Later I found out that Jean Hagen, the actor playing Lina Lamont, had the good voice, the better one, and it was her voice they used when Debbie Reynolds pretended it was her voice pretending to be Lina's. The dubbing had been dubbed back to source.

I was never sure what there was to learn from this, but now it strikes me as a pretty good definition of poetry. You start out silent, then borrow someone else's voice and try to fit it to your mouth. It doesn't work. You keep trying until finally – yes! – there it is: you have your own voice.

But now it's the mouth that's no longer yours.

THE COOLING TOWERS OF DIDCOT

It was the inattentive eye that saw them best:
breeze-block vases with their tapered waists,
their smoky pouts. They were modest,

middle-distant; they had the permanence
of grey things: seen but rarely noticed;
or, if noticed, only once.

When the dynamite sapped them, a ripple
climbed their flanks; their mouths
were trying to say something difficult.

They hesitated, as if falling was a choice,
and when they fell they sleeved
their outlines, peeled themselves

off the air that wouldn't quite let them go,
that even seemed to try to hold them up.
They did their best to go unnoticed, even now,

though crowds had gathered: the local news,
a man who worked there and thought them beautiful,
who cried in the same reticent way they fell,

and the developers whose view they'd blocked.
Then they crashed silently into smoke and dust
followed by their noise which arrived too late.

★

I miss them – their uninsistent presence:
sometimes it felt like they were moving
and we were not; from Didcot station's

interzone, they looked serene,
brewing clouds in concrete stills;
in our connecting-train hypnosis,

they were the ones who seemed to leave,
weighed anchors and steamboat chimneys,
and we who stayed behind; their smoky *sillage*

seen through a rainy window
was part of the commuting consciousness,
those small realistic dreams

that visit when we doze in public places;
the porous ones that use ingredients
from the world around and fold them in

to our brief, matt fantasies of escape:
nothing extreme or too destabilising;
more like liquid on a not-quite-flat surface,

always edging slightly across its borders
but never over-spilling. They promised
that the ordinary would always quietly

exceed its confines but never break them down.
That it was inexhaustible; ever-grey plains
of everyday things, so many and so much

that you didn't need to look, not now at any rate,
because it would always be there.
You could pay attention next time,

and there would always be a next time.
So for now you let them slide
into the margins of your need to be somewhere,

the burned-off vapour of your hurry
in the return journey of water becoming air
becoming water.

Now they're gone
there's only the pragmatic little station
to which they seemed to say:

you have the timetables but we have the time.

THE NOISES THINGS MAKE
WHEN THEY LEAVE

Connoisseur of the noises things make when they leave:
the clip of heels on pavements,
the suitcases on rubber wheels;
a station pigeon's piebald underwing,

the bike-chain's sticky grind.
A car chews through the gears.
A train burns away to cable-sparks.
The ferries clear their foghorn throats.

There are so many ways of going yet you stay.

FACTORY TOWN

The factory closed and the days,
once serried and distinct,
bled into each other like sleep hours.

The week became a distillation
of all our Sundays.
As mornings ran aground

on empty afternoons we found
that everything we called ourselves,
our distinctness, was invested

in contingent things:
a factory and some shops,
and beyond them, faraway shares

and tradeable bonds, a world away
from the oil and the grease and the table beer;
we found that being who we were

wasn't some mysterious thing that we were gifted,
the mix of luck and fortitude
we call a class, a nation or a people,

but an arrangement of someone else's numbers
two continents away.
In the slackened tether of its moorings

the place we thought we lived in
emigrated, and it was we who stayed behind.
The rope unbraided into twine,

the twine separated into string,
the string became a thread.
We didn't know how thinly it all hung,

how quickly gone;
or how the edge was always near;
now that the edge is here.

TRAVELODGE

You wonder who designs these places.
You find them off roundabouts,
after circumlocutions of motorway.
They are a way of never getting to the point.

Perhaps you have an interview nearby,
and that is why you drove here, this reef
of dormitory coral on the outskirts of a town that looks
just like the one you left.

Perhaps you have no more interviews, and that is why.

Perhaps you're reapplying for your old job
as a husband or a wife, a mother or a father,
or for a new one as the same, in a start-up
where your skill-set is required.

Maybe the start-up's you.

You've packed a half-bottle of something strong,
proof against sleeping badly or too well;
you settle like the coffee granules in the single-
portion sachets in the breakfast room.

Even in the slow race to the bottom of yourself
you seem to have come last.
The mirror watches you unpack
your endless shallow bag,
its well of lonely clothes.

The television is a furnace burning local news.

You are breathing wardrobe-air.

The plastic kettle rages and wants to know who's there.

FIRST OF THE LAST GOODBYES

I wonder which it was: the first of the last
goodbyes. I wonder if we knew it by its taste
and if one kiss stands out for how it started
autumn in our mouths.

I wonder when it was we smelt
the spores of damp inside the new-build
house we thought we'd made; or saw the crazing
in the paint that opened to the plaster crack
that soon would rift with brick-dust and then air.

I wonder when it came, and wonder why it is
that time won't bring us back the perfect strangers
we began as: when everything was different,
and everything the same,

and everything unhappening at once.

BLOOD FEATHER

The noise of a punched cushion,
then a ghost against the glass:
a pigeon's outline in feather-dust,
the ridged, plume-detail of its hologram.

In films the spirit leaves the body
still contoured to what it was:
a trick of the camera that feeds
the mind's own tricks,
shows us other surfaces
where we live on.

The blood feather leaks
like a broken nib;
the puckered eyelids close;
the claws curl in, the holding tight
that is the letting go;
the next rain against the window.

LANDLINE

It grew in the hallway beside the pot-plant,
the ashtray, and the *Yellow Pages* left ajar.
It started under floorboards, unspooled
between the carpets and their waferings of underlay.

It tracked the skirtings, spined down corners,
knew the smell of slippers, insoles crumbling
at the heel or toe; it knew the frayed shadows
that we threw: the address book's fading numbers

and the crossed-out friends; the names trussed up
in angry biro or speared by one calm line of ink;
the half-there, the less-and-less . . . the care home
'Hotline' and the ads for stairlifts, window-cleaners, take-aways.

It finished in an A5 sheet blu-tak'd to the wall:
IMPORTANT NUBERS [sic] with the contacts
for their children, two nurses, and the remnants
of a family one continent away: +00 32 *etc.*

The dead lines outgrew the living, the A to Z
went back to A again, an alphabet in countdown,
until what remained when we had cleared the house
was the polished square where the phone had sat,

framed in dust, pieces of skin or dandruff at the edges,
milled to something that felt like talc.
Last to go was the word we called it by: *landline*,
exotic as a telegram. Our fingers tracked

it underground, getting mustier, earthier, fungal
at the seams where our houses let the outside in;
with the woodlice and the silverfish,
the bluebottles stripped for parts on windowsills:

the phone, the flex, the pigtail-coil
where we made our rings and knuckledusters
as we talked; the receiver that got hot against our ears,
the plughole-glug of someone hanging up

that was the echo of our listening; the last word,
the good news and the bad, there in the hallway,
where we fiddled with whatever we could find,
where there was never a pen that worked,

a pencil that had lead in, before our telephones
lived on air; before we called them landlines.

THE WAVE

I crossed the ring road on a bony metal footbridge
that shivered in the wind. To Littlemore.
The name sounds like a plea. It begs.
A name on bended knee. Increments of wanting,
of not getting. Thirty years in Oxford
and I'd never been – to the road
where two asylums meet.

The sun is going down fighting
as the lady in slippers and pyjamas
with the overcoat for smoking outside in all weathers
stands at the open gates, their keeper and their kept.

Mistaking for a wave the hand I raise
to shield my eyes, she waves to me:
a regal, medicalised screenwipe of her palm.

I must wave back because the first time didn't count.
I wasn't waving. Now I am, so now she waves again.
I'll always be one wave behind and as I try to gain on her,
each wave takes me further back

until, crossing this suburban gulf,

I'm waving to my mother;
we're outside Tooting hospital,
it's twenty years ago,
she smokes and rolls her cigarettes
and sees me coming and she waves:
a recognition-scene across the mirror-line of decades,
played out to sirens and the beep of key-fobs.

★

Later, I'm at home; she is in the strip-lit
common room among the jigsaws,
facing the sound-down TV.

The wave goes on; we were just the way it moved.

PROSE BETWEEN STATIONS

Things seen/heard from the top floor of the Brussels/Luxembourg Inter-City Express (only the train is fast – life inside and out takes place in some other zone of time, as thickly weightless as footage of an astronaut cooking breakfast between planets):

At Ciney, a bull nonchalantly mounting a cow (this is outside the train) as the cow

grazes on, pestling mouthfuls of grass with a slow swing of her jaw. She chews in time to his slack thrusts, each one hovering effortfully at the edges of itself, as if pulling into and out of Velcro. This is the middle-distance, with neither the prestige of the faraway nor the imperiousness of foreground. The whole scene depends on the train's speed, which allows the traveller, forehead laid refreshingly against the glass, to pick it out with a distinctness and granularity that is at first disproportionate to its interest, but which quickly becomes its interest.

At Ottignies, students from Louvain-la-Neuve climb aboard with backpacks full of laundry for their mothers to wash: a journey of twenty minutes undertaken with a month of clothing. They are equipped to emigrate, but instead descend, as they always do, twenty minutes later, at Gembloux, where

three workmen off the day shift at a zinc-plating factory step on and talk about their friend who hanged himself yesterday, the evening of the burial of his wife, dead last month of a pulmonary thrombosis. At Namur,

three kindergarten teachers replace them seat for seat, discuss the school's Christmas decorations, affectionately mention a troublesome boy they like but whose life is in danger of going . . . one of them searches for the right phrase then, with a little laugh, gestures around her and says with a sort of embarrassed satisfaction, *off the rails* . . . then settle down

44

to comparing different brands of sleeping tablet with the discrimination and adjectival range of sommeliers discussing vintages.

The sky is a mild, uniform grey, streaked with oily-looking damp like those antimacassars in old people's homes.

This raw material thinks of all the contortions it would have to go through to become a poem, and decides to stay as it is: nondescript, if not undescribed.

GHOST-STATIONS

I Bruxelles-Congrès/Brussel-Congres

It's now an out-take, a special number of a station,
closed at weekends 'to help disengorge the network'*:
but still the trains pass through it, run it through,

reminding us how quickly these days we produce Oblivion,
how fast we waste, how obsolescence more and more
comes neck and neck with what it obsolesces

and soon may come before it. It probably already has.

* 'Pour nous aider à désengorger le réseau': Found poetry from the SNCB
spokeswoman.

II Bruxelles-Chapelle/Brussel-Kapellekerk

This is the deadest of the *gares-fantômes* : deadest
because so freshly dead: renovated first and then sealed up,
embalmed in €uros, a skatepark sarcophagus of graffiti.
In this undercountry, it's not ghosts who pass through us,
cold crossings of mortality, but we who pass

through them, threading the spectres with our bodies.
The buskers have moved on, the commuters moved away,
the *waffel* stands have climbed above the ground:
all are blinking in the light that they half-know,
returning from the half-light they knew best.

DOORS AND WINDOWS OF WALLONIA

Before television backlit them with its haunted blues,
its gauze of voice over voice, dubbings of *Dynasty* and *Dallas*,
there were firesides filtered through net curtains, shadows
pulling free from shadows. The furniture didn't furnish,
it loomed; heavy as cannon, it boomed darkness.

After closedown, after the trembling not-quite-stasis
of the *RTB* testcard, the blue glow lingered,
fizzed against mosquito nets, caught the flypaper garlands
with their incrustation of bluebottle and *mouche à merde*,
the banal shitfly with his coalface glitter.

That was the house's pulse, a comatose cellar-beat
to which my grandmother, Bouillon's only dressmaker,
pedalled kilometres of stitching, threaded her needles
seven to seven in daylight that took all day to die.
Her only books were swatches; she held them up

to the daughters and widows of Wallonia
fresh with their ideas from Brussels, of *haute couture*,
their cut-outs from *Paris-Match*: a small-town catwalk
of Deneuves along a corridor of Stockman mannequins
stuck with pins, stained with oil or grease, and for me then

(for me still) so oddly sexual with their tapered waists,
the perfection of their closedness. My face at the window, I'd watch
her busy sparrow-jerks inside the darkness that fleshed her out,
and smell the last-but-one all-day *pot-au-feu* that held its own
against the clashing scents of factory-owners' wives.

But the body that stays caught in the full-length looking-glass
is mine, my drowning childhood pulling down, and these days
nothing – least of all my whole life – flashes by. Only the empty

mirror gives me back that time, and the lace curtains,
more air than lace, are sieves for shadows to pass through light.

Each time I breathe I breathe it in, that sublimate of all that's gone.
Essence of Indoors would be the perfume, if they made it.

FRONTIER CAFÉS

from the French of Gilles Ortlieb

There are no more mines in Volmerange-les-mines;
no cinema either, despite the *Café du Ciné*
offering chairs to sit out on the terrace,
weather permitting. On the way out of town,
past the last of the houses, the *No Man's Land*
is face-to-face with *L'Entre-deux*, a former customs hut
now converted into a chip stall on the other side
of the country road: the frontier is close by,
barely two hundred metres
and ten years away. I stopped
because of the name, pulled up a chair in the gravel
to watch the line of shadow slowly stretch
along the tarmac: a quiet homage
to the *entre-deux* I've sentenced myself to,
stumbling between now and there, between here
and then, still hesitating between me and me.

THE NEW SHOPPING CENTRE

The cranes have gone. The Westgate after rain
gleams under a pigeon-spike tiara.
Today they fit the cash machines,
the shelves, the final laminated glass vitrines.

A van unloads a charnel-house of mannequins.
A box of heads with faces closed; a box of hands
of which half beckon, half refuse. Then info-panels:
'Learn about the vanished suburb of St Ebbe's'

and 'Trill-Mill Lane in History'. They've kept the names.
That's nice. The places? Landfill. Archaeo-yesterday.
Money, like the rain, will always find the shortest way.

The verb *to vanish* fills the holes on which we stand.
The corporate Ozymandias surveys
his honeycombing galleries of brands.

TOFFS AND TOUGHS

There's a dovecote, tidy as a dollhouse,
on the third-floor balcony of our street's last slice
of council flats: perspex side-walls and little porches

where thoroughbred pigeons air their plumes
and live their show-home lives. Dieted and groomed,
they take supplements, wear ankle rings, have names.

On the railing opposite the city pigeons eye them up.
They eat shavings of kebab and kerbside macerations
of burger baps and rain. Their feathers are greasy,

lubed with bin-juice and exhaust-fume slick,
and their necks when they turn and catch the light
are the rainbows in petrol-station puddles.

Their bubble-gum claws are ringless, stumped
at the knuckle; leprous, cropped and nobbled.
Some have punctured eyes and threadbare tails

from scrapes with cats. They have a ragged
irony about them, a streetside-swagger
as they lounge and watch their overbred cousins

gentrify the air. They're on opposite ends
of what it is to be the same, like the famous photo
of posh schoolboys outside Lord's, with their top hats,

carnations, canes; while the local kids, mitching
from school, more curious than envious,
peer at them across the species gulf that isn't one,

from the other side of nature that's all nurture.

THE PLAIN

The fountain on The Plain beside the roundabout
about which there's nothing much to say except

it used to be a tollbooth that used to be a church
that used to be a cemetery whose bones

still pick their way back up each time the council
digs for pipes or cables. That fountain.

With the water that ran out when.
And the clock that's always then.

The nervy weathervane that shows
you where the wind's just been, not where it blows.

The Latin motto says the only time you need
to know about is time that rhymes with tide:

LYMPHA CADIT   RUIT HORA
SAGAX BIBE   CARPE FUGACEM

The water sinks   the hour flows
the wise drink   seize what goes.

III

AFTER THE FLOOD

a journey in diversions

We go leaving ourselves all over —
in beds, in rooms, in fields, in seas, in cities —
and each of those fragments
that has stopped being us goes on
as always being us

Silvina Ocampo

Returning in a time of plague and flood,
I am diverted, with this train,
into the lining of my country,
making notes in a receipt book
from the hardware shelf of *Delhaize Proxy*.

Each word has its counterfoil,
its carbon double, on the page beneath.
It's the anniversary of my mother's death,
and my mother's birthday –
the day she short-circuited the tenses,
made the current flow both ways.

Diversion I: Brussels-Midi to Villiers-Ville

Détournement/Wegomlegging :
big words, small distances: cross-hatches
of tracks and sidings, *calques* of local traffic;
cropped vistas beneath the grey, meat-marbling sky.
What land I can still see looks borrowed from the water.

Two swans, escaped from a nearby poem about Bruges,
ride their caramel reflections among the gargling bins.

★

Between stops we are learning a new tense:
notebook-time, between the written
and the yet to write, the invoice
and the proof of payment,
as the passing station-names –
faint through the maculated window –
cast spells from the timetable's grimoire:
the fade-out that is the grammar

of my grief, spreading like a verb
through its declensions.

I tell my rosary of *gares désaffectées*,
ghost-stations that haunt the line
long after they've been closed;
places so familiar they capsize
and become exotic once again.

I see them for the first time
and the last time all in one.
The greeting and the valediction
have swallowed everything between.

*

Diversion grafted onto diversion;
the ever-ramifying journey back;
the points change; a new track.

Diversion II: Profondeville

Head against cold glass, I am joined
at the temple by my mirror-twin.
We share a daydream of toy trains
undulating through toy towns:
green-sponge hedgerows, toothpick fences,
paper-maché gardens with pipe-cleaner trees.

Our talent was for reducing things,
small miracles of scale: matchbox
shop-fronts, bilingual streets,
frayed pennants for Anderlecht and Union Saint-Gilloise.
Then the bathos of local match-days

at Standard de Bouillon: the games
slugged out in fat wet kicks
to an aura of small-town grudge.
We built the under-attended stadium,
down to the goalposts' ochre rust.

You painted the dark windows
of the house with the shouting in;
the domestic interior and its bleed;
an ambulance.

I wanted to see the siren flash,
hear the urgent spiral of its scream
that made me think of speed,
of corners turned, of anywhere but here.

Diversion III: 'En partance'

I chose the InterCity, the straight lines,
wanted to see the capitals, feel the land
fast-forward across the filler-towns
we came from. You liked it to unspool
like cassette-tape, in looping,
chewed-up coils of place.

Your aversion to short-cuts:
une perte de temps, you said,
a waste of time.

You always took the long way home –
that was your time regained.

★

Choosing seats at Libramont
you faced backwards so you could see
what you had missed,
watch the going thinning to the gone.

It's how we face each other still,
touching in some crossing of the light
where anticipation and retrospect align.

★

At Mechelen/Malines, the place-names fold
across the mirror-line of languages.
Then Brussels started in allotments
banking up the railway track;
the flash of greenhouse-panes,
their pale reverberating suns.

Avenue de Stalingrad, Palais du Midi,
streets that rinsed the colours down to grey;
the tooth-mugs rattling above the sinks
of the one-star hotels on Boulevard Lemonnier.

Diversion IV – Jemeppe Reservoirs

Behind the tapestry of connectivity,
in a time of Covid, after floods,
a time of masks and vaccine passes,
the cast-off rails are rusting
and the sleepers lie like matchsticks
as the new track glitters with its fitted-kitchen shine.

Soon only the cities will talk,
the way high-tech household gadgets

communicate across the spaces
where crumbs gather and the bodies leak.

We are the provincial slack,
we are the static on the line.

J'prends le local : I'll take the local train.
You let me have the capitals,
you took the diversion every time.

Diversion V - Fleurus

The missed connection, unstitch in time:
one mis-step in homage to you
and a portal opens in the timetable –
a code known only to those who miss their trains,
discovering how the small town shows itself,
botanical in the way it opens out.

Time not as river but as estuary:
its drain and glut, the taut, the slack;
nothing gained or lost; a ridge of drying welter
where the water is yet to filter back.

Diversion VI - Sambreville

Listening to the stuck record I have become
I wonder, am I the stylus or the vinyl?
(Your answer: I am the scratch.)

Waiting for the points to change,
caught in the endless way it ends.

Diversion VII: Floreffe to Malonne

The trees are drawn like curtains across the track.
For fifteen minutes we are the forest's memory
of the days before the cities came to eat it up,
the speed-read pages of the Ardennes dreambook.

I entered with a mouthful of French
– piercing in the ears, the bends –
and I came out in English.

Diversion VIII: Charleroi Outskirts

I only need to see the windows
to know who lives there, how they fill
the thickness of the shadows;
how it smells, the swell of wallpaper
crispy-damp in the microclimate
of some dead shop's display.

In the corridors, aromas
of the last three meals,
each one a tense all to itself:
if I could describe how it all holds
I'd have the words for all I need.
I'll find the lining where it's all kept
so long as I manage the old trick,
my only trick: arriving just in time
to see myself arrive too late.

★

The anniversaries are the beads
we thread with our returns.

Diversion IX – Libramont to Bertrix

The trains still hesitate as they pass through
the stations where they once stopped,
as if the track still flexed some muscle-memory
among stalled wheels and rusty pumps,
slack catenaries and chain-link fences.

Ghost-letters, whispers of old businesses,
the dream-language of the faded signs:
the factory-towns clocked in, the factory-towns
bleed out, into something like the tense
I had such hopes for: fading as resistance,
these propagated cuttings of the past.

*

Memory: my anchor and my wreck,
my future-burning archive, my fossil fuel;
no carbon-neutral way of going back,
no long way home, no sidewise time
with which to fill my clock.

Diversion X – Arrival

It's not so much a thought,
distinct with edges
and abutting other thoughts,
as a swelling on the line
between then and now,
slow as this clotted network,
as the water-table rising:

I wonder if this is still a poem,
and if it even wants to be;
if it prefers to stay behind
in the notebook it began in –
remembered for how it came,
lines in a rice-paper *carnet*
not where it finished up,
here in a book –

how *ceci n'est pas un poème*, and how it is,
and how I dragged it across languages to make it so.

★

These notes on carbon sheets on which I've pressed too hard,
their imprint now three pages deep:
with elegies our words should be the tidemark not the tide.

ACKNOWLEDGEMENTS

Several of these poems appeared in the following publications: *Edinburgh Review*, *London Review of Books*, *PN Review* and the *Times Literary Supplement*.

'The Cooling Towers of Didcot' was first broadcast on BBC Radio 3's *The Verb* in November 2020.